SAFE BY DESIGN

SAFE
SPORTS EQUIPMENT

by Kaitlyn Duling

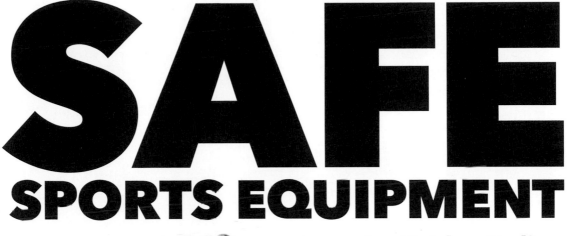

pogo

Ideas for Parents and Teachers

Pogo Books let children practice reading informational text while introducing them to nonfiction features such as headings, labels, sidebars, maps, and diagrams, as well as a table of contents, glossary, and index.

Carefully leveled text with a strong photo match offers early fluent readers the support they need to succeed.

Before Reading

- "Walk" through the book and point out the various nonfiction features. Ask the student what purpose each feature serves.
- Look at the glossary together. Read and discuss the words.

Read the Book

- Have the child read the book independently.
- Invite him or her to list questions that arise from reading.

After Reading

- Discuss the child's questions. Talk about how he or she might find answers to those questions.
- Prompt the child to think more. Ask: Why is it so important to wear the right equipment when you play sports?

Pogo Books are published by Jump!
5357 Penn Avenue South
Minneapolis, MN 55419
www.jumplibrary.com

Copyright © 2020 Jump!
International copyright reserved in all countries.
No part of this book may be reproduced in any form without written permission from the publisher.

Library of Congress Cataloging-in-Publication Data

Names: Duling, Kaitlyn, author.
Title: Safe sports equipment / by Kaitlyn Duling.
Description: Minneapolis, MN : Jump!, Inc., [2020]
Series: Safe by design | Audience: Age 7-10.
Includes index.
Identifiers: LCCN 2018056986 (print)
LCCN 2018060100 (ebook)
ISBN 9781641288804 (ebook)
ISBN 9781641288781 (hardcover : alk. paper)
ISBN 9781641288798 (pbk.)
Subjects: LCSH: Children's accidents—Prevention—Juvenile literature. | Sports—Safety measures—Juvenile literature.
Classification: LCC HV675.5 (ebook)
LCC HV675.5 .D85 2020 (print)
DDC 688.7028/9—dc23
LC record available at https://lccn.loc.gov/2018056986

Editor: Susanne Bushman
Designer: Anna Peterson

Photo Credits: Supertrooper/Dreamstime, cover; Sergey Novikov/Shutterstock, 1; akova/iStock, 3; Scott Sanders/Shutterstock, 4; Steve Debenport/iStock, 5, 12; A_Lesik/Shutterstock, 6-7; indigolotos/Shutterstock, 8 (left); tescha555/Shutterstock, 8 (right); Levranii/Shutterstock, 9; Radius Images/Getty, 10-11; Andrey_Popov/Shutterstock, 13; Eugene_Onischenko/iStock, 14-15; Oleksandr Osipov/Shutterstock, 16-17; vm/iStock, 18-19; Chelsea Purgahn/AP Images, 20-21; monticello/Shutterstock, 23.

Printed in the United States of America at Corporate Graphics in North Mankato, Minnesota.

TABLE OF CONTENTS

CHAPTER 1
Made for Safety..................................4

CHAPTER 2
Keep Your Head in the Game...............8

CHAPTER 3
Winning Gear..............................12

ACTIVITIES & TOOLS
Try This!....................................22
Glossary...................................23
Index.......................................24
To Learn More...........................24

CHAPTER 1

MADE FOR SAFETY

Can you imagine soccer without shin guards? What about football without helmets? Sports can be dangerous.

shin guard

Without safety gear, athletes can get hurt. These injuries can be painful.

Contact sports are intense. Players **tackle**. They hit. They crash. They can get hit by balls, pucks, and more.

Engineers design **equipment**. It lowers the **impact** of these hits. We wear special items for each sport. Helmets, pads, guards, and shoes keep us safe.

DID YOU KNOW?

Helmets, pads, and guards are not new. Warriors wore them in ancient Rome and Greece! They were made of metal.

CHAPTER 2

KEEP YOUR HEAD IN THE GAME

Helmets are the most important sports equipment. Why? They protect your **skull** and brain. They **absorb** impact.

What happens without a helmet? Your skull and brain absorb the impact. This can cause a **concussion**. Ouch!

Football players did not always wear helmets. They did not come into play until the early 1940s. The first ones were made of leather.

Today's helmets are stronger. Some have **sensors**. They can record impacts. Special materials can absorb more **energy**.

TAKE A LOOK!

Helmets have many parts. Each part has a job.

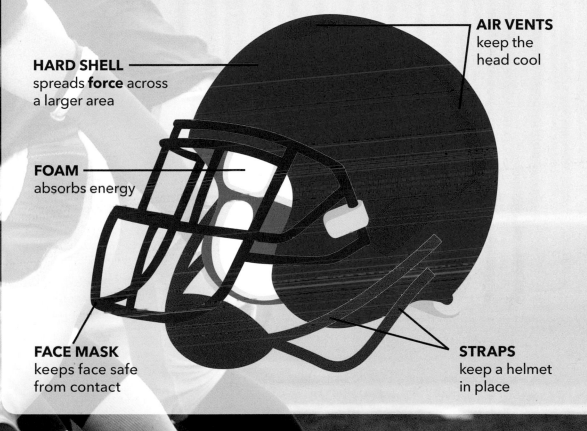

AIR VENTS
keep the head cool

HARD SHELL
spreads **force** across a larger area

FOAM
absorbs energy

FACE MASK
keeps face safe from contact

STRAPS
keep a helmet in place

CHAPTER 3

WINNING GEAR

Swimmers wear goggles. Hockey players wear face masks. Even golfers have special gear. Gloves protect hands from blisters.

glove · · · · ▶

Engineers study injuries. They look at how they are caused. Then they look for ways to prevent them. This might mean adding more cushion to shoes.

Professional football players hit hard. Pads and guards keep their shoulders and collarbones safe. Pads and guards are made to fit each player.

DID YOU KNOW?

Some sports require special gear. Boaters wear life vests. These float. Gymnasts wear grips on their hands. Wrestlers wear helmets to cover their ears.

Soccer players race down the field. Their shoes have **cleats**. These grip the grass. They give better control. They help prevent ankle **sprains**.

Other sports have special shoes, too. Basketball and volleyball sneakers have good **traction**. This keeps players' shoes from slipping on the court.

DID YOU KNOW?

Some bicyclists wear cleats. These clip into the pedals. Energy transfers to the bike more easily. Bicyclists can go faster!

cleat ·····▶

Check! Hockey players slam into each other. This can cause injuries. Engineers updated pads to help. How? They added foam to shoulder pads.

TAKE A LOOK!

Hockey goalies wear large pads and helmets. Why? These protect them from flying pucks!

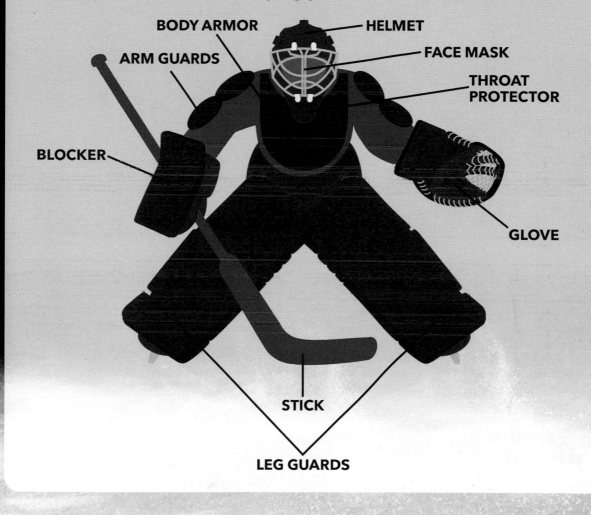

BODY ARMOR

ARM GUARDS

HELMET

FACE MASK

THROAT PROTECTOR

BLOCKER

GLOVE

STICK

LEG GUARDS

It is game day! We gear up.
Not sure what to wear?
Ask your coach. Stay safe.
Then you can focus on fun!

ACTIVITIES & TOOLS

EGG HELMET

Helmets are designed to keep your brain from getting hurt. In this activity, design a helmet to keep an egg from cracking!

What You Need:
- one carton of eggs
- scissors
- masking tape
- old newspapers
- plastic bags
- cardboard tubes
- straws
- a short ladder (and an adult to help)

❶ Use your materials to design a helmet or guards and pads for your egg that will keep it from breaking when dropped.

❷ Go outside. Set up your ladder on a flat surface. Now drop your egg from four feet (1.2 meters) above the ground. What happens? Does the egg break?

❸ If the egg broke, try a new design. Record your results. Which materials and designs lessen the impact on the egg?

GLOSSARY

absorb: To take in or soak up.

cleats: Small, pointed shapes on the bottom of shoes.

concussion: A brain injury that causes temporary loss of normal brain function.

contact sports: Sports in which athletes come into physical contact with one another.

energy: The ability of something to do work.

engineers: People who design systems, structures, products, or machines.

equipment: The tools or products needed for a particular purpose, such as a sport.

force: Strength or energy that, once exerted, causes a change in motion.

impact: The forceful striking of one thing against another.

sensors: Instruments that can detect and measure changes and transmit the information to a controlling device.

skull: The hard, boney covering around one's brain.

sprains: Stretches or tears of tissues, causing swelling, bruising, and pain.

tackle: To knock or throw a player to the ground.

traction: A state of tension or grip.

INDEX

cleats 16

coach 20

concussion 9

contact sports 7

energy 10, 11, 16

engineers 7, 13, 18

equipment 7, 8

face mask 11, 12, 19

football 4, 10, 15

gloves 12, 19

golfers 12

helmets 4, 7, 8, 9, 10, 11, 15, 19

hockey players 12, 18, 19

impact 7, 8, 9, 10

injuries 5, 13, 18

sensors 10

shin guards 4

shoes 7, 13, 16

shoulder pads 15, 18

skull 8, 9

soccer 4, 16

traction 16

TO LEARN MORE

Finding more information is as easy as 1, 2, 3.

❶ Go to www.factsurfer.com

❷ Enter "safesportsequipment" into the search box.

❸ Choose your cover to see a list of websites.